Pocketbook
of
Affirmations

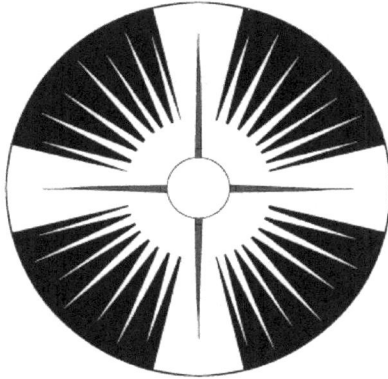

Tools for Transformation

Betty Lue Lieber, Ph.D. MFT

ISBN: 978-0-9899133-1-7

Printed in the United States of America

Reunion Press
17664 Greenridge Road
Hidden Valley Lake, CA 95467

Other books by Betty Lue Lieber, PhD, MFT

Loving Reminders 2000, 2014

Peaceful Reminders 2001, 2014

Relationship Reminders 2003, 2012

Healing Reminders 2014

Healthy Reminders 2014

Family Reminders 2014

Dedication

I am dedicating this book to all those who seek a better way.
The family of humanity calls for a change.

When we change our thoughts, we change our words.
When we change our words, we can change our behavior.
In every change, there is transformation of relationships.
In this time of transformation, we can create consciously.

I give this book to you who want to make a difference.
I dedicate my writing to you who want to find a better way.
I write these affirmations to undo limited habits of mind.
I share what I know with those who seek affirmative reminders.

This book is a gift to me from the Love that created me.
Life is a gift of Love for us and given to us to use for Love.
Affirmations are one way to remember this Love!
We are here to be Loving affirming reminders for one another.

Betty Lue

Contents

Preface

We are responsible for the words we speak.
We are responsible for the experiences we have.
Thoughts and beliefs, words, written and spoken, create.
We are often unaware of unconscious programming.
We need to clear our limiting thoughts and beliefs.

Affirmations clear the limiting beliefs and negativity.
Affirmations undo what is not true.
Affirmations, correctly used, set us free to choose again.
Affirmations awaken our minds to trust and freedom.

Use affirmations to clear past programming.
Use affirmations to recognize programmed blocks.
Use affirmations to free your mind from learned limitations.
Use affirmations to open your mind to inner guidance.

Let us use affirmations to change our lives.
Let us use affirmations as tools for transformation.
Let us use affirmations to be all we can be.
Let us use affirmations to transform our world.

Betty Lue

Acknowledgments

Affirmations flow from my quiet Mind and Open Heart, where I listen to the Voice Within, the Holy Spirit, that lives within each one of us.

Thank you Spirit.

You, the readers, have been my inspiration, my reason, and my encouragement for putting them into book form.

Thank you Friends.

My Life Partner, Robert Waldon, is my helpmate and support in bringing the printed form to you with spiritual integrity.

Thank you Robert.

I am forever grateful to the Love that lives within us and sets us free to totally trust in the Love We Are together.

Thank you Love.

Introduction

This is a book of affirmations. It is powerful in its intention, for it will clear your mind to see who you really are. In truly recognizing ourselves, we experience health, happiness and peace of mind.

Affirmations contain truth which frees the mind from faulty thinking. The mental computer stores in its memory the data we put in. It does not discriminate between truth and illusion and receives whatever it is given and seems to fit with its current programming or beliefs.

This is a book designed to assist you in times of uncertainty and fear and to help you return to a sense of joyful confidence and peace.

The positive thoughts within this book are to bring to mind the Truth about your Self, the Highest and Best within you. It is only the **mistaken** belief in your lack and limitation that has kept you feeling small and separate from your Wholeness.

Transformation occurs in you, as you release your past learned beliefs, and open to the present Truth about your Self.

You are Infinite in Beauty, Wisdom and Love.

You are as you were created = Perfect.

You went to sleep, went unconscious, and forgot your True Source, the Essence in you.

You will now easily remember who you truly are.

 It is fun, safe and easy to affirm and appreciate One's Self.

Truths

1. *Thought creates.*
2. *Each thought I think and each word I speak creates a result.*
3. *Unconscious mind-chatter is merely programming from the past.*
4. *I release my limited thinking by consciously choosing expansive and affirming thoughts.*

Ideas For Using Affirmations

1. Use the positive thought which is opposite of your limited or negative belief.
2. Use your name in the affirmation whenever possible.
3. Repeat the affirmation aloud as you write it ten to twenty times a day minimum.
4. It is easy to sing or record affirmations for further repetitions.

Positive thoughts act as loving erasers for the fearfulness and limitation we accepted in the past.

You now accept only those thoughts that add to your life; the rest is easily released forever.

I recommend taking care of survival, security and safety needs first.

I suggest that you find a place, a time, a person and/or a method of returning to a state of love and gratitude.

In our natural state of love and gratitude (inner peace), our resources, inner guidance, clarity of vision, direction and focus are all available, creating more simplicity and peace for me and for you.

The Power Of Affirmation

Your thought, word and action are your power. Words are constantly either building or tearing down, healing or destroying. You can now choose words for your Highest Good. Use your name in each one. Use your name when you affirm what is your Divine right.

Be willing to do affirmations; they're fun! Affirmations are a safe and easy way to choose for freedom. The simple truth about affirmations is that they work.

These affirmations are all designed to assist you in clearing away false beliefs, mistaken learnings, and limitations of your Self. The purpose of these affirmations is to bring you to a state of peace, inner joy, and Divine Love. They have been given to me to share with you.

Remember that there is power in the word. Therefore, choose your words wisely. Remember that what you ask for you receive, exactly as you have asked. Remember that in every word, energy is expressing itself through you. So, choose your words with simple innocence and wisdom.

Affirmations lovingly release any false beliefs of lack, limitation or littleness which you may have learned in your life. Every place where you have judged yourself calls to be erased (released) so that you might be free to express your magnificence with love and joy.

Affirmations are to be "high" enough and "clear" enough to reverse the thinking that is present. In a state of Love, our thoughts and words are creative, inspiring, an extension of goodness, beauty and wholeness.

Loving Affirmations

The following pages contain sample affirmations for most areas of your life.

You may use these as they are.

You may wish to modify specific affirmations to better apply to your circumstances.

Lastly, you may find that these affirmations awaken in you an awareness of specific thoughts which need healing and for which you can create your own personal affirmation.

We encourage you to write your changes and additions directly in the book.

Personal Growth

- I like my Authentic Self.

- I trust my Self.

- I no longer trust decisions made in fear and anger.

- I trust choices made in Love for the sake of Love.

- I no longer judge or resist what others say.

- I freely speak the Truth, and trust it serves all.

- I trust what I say in joy and love.

- I give my life to good, and I am aware of the Good in me.

- I love my Self-discovery process.

- I enjoy every minute I spend with my Self.

- My forgiveness and gratitude heal all things.

- I now treat my Self with sensitivity and respect.

- I meet all fear with love, and every fear resolves and dissolves.

Communication

- I am now willing to tell the truth without anger, fear or guilt.

- I no longer hold back; I freely share my Self and my experience.

- I am willing to release all embarrassment and say what is appropriate in every situation.

- I am willing to be a channel for good news and love.

- I now communicate my thoughts and feelings with joy and ease.

- I create a consistent and clear intention to heal every problem.

- I now communicate fully and freely.

  I am willing to be honest and open.

- I am willing to see the love which transcends all anger.

- I am willing to see the love which transcends all fear.

- I communicate my needs clearly and on purpose.

- I ask for help when I need to be reminded that I am "OK".

- I remember that my purpose is to heal when I communicate.

- I am always communicating with thought, word and deed, so I choose to communicate love with my life.

- The more I give love and forgiveness with every thought, word and deed, the more I experience love in every relationship.

Choice

- I now choose to play the game of life to a joyous win for all.

- I gladly support and encourage my Self to do exactly what I want to do.

- I take care of my Whole Self first; therefore, I always have an abundance of love to give.

- I now choose thoughts (affirmations) which are truly Best for my Highest Good.

- Everything I want, I have; therefore, I choose only that which is Best for me.

- I know what I truly want, and I accept it with gratitude.

- I choose what I want to see.

- I am what I choose to be. I now choose what is best for me.

- I do what brings me joy and feel good about it.

- I deserve to joyfully spend money on myself and others.

- I have exactly what I want and I am satisfied.

- I am alone only when I choose to be alone.

- I choose wisely.

- I know what is right and good for me.

- I always know what I'm doing.

- Anything I do that is best for me will be best for everyone.

- I choose to think, act, and express only the good, the beautiful and the Whole.

- Every negative thought I think is quickly and consciously replaced by the perfect positive one.

- I choose to live fully.

- I choose to breathe freely.
- I choose to have life and have it more and more abundantly.
- I choose laughter and love as a remedy for pain and sorrow.
- I choose love for that is what I am.
- I choose peace for it brings me rest.

For Another

- I love you.

- I believe in you.

- I trust your life process.

- I experience God working in you and through you.

- I wholly support your happiness, aliveness and freedom.

- I see you beautiful, good and whole (holy).

- I may not always agree with what you do; however, I am willing to trust in you and your right to choose for yourself.

- I trust you to grow in your own way, in your own time.

- I hold the vision of your holiness.

- I know you are a creation of God.

- I trust in our joined purpose to see the Highest Truth in each other.

- I see your perfection.

- You are created in His likeness and Image.

- I see the light of God radiating through you.

- You are loved. You are blessed because you are Divine.

- I free myself and you of all past judgments, pain and fear. I set you free to be.

- I am the mirror in which you see yourself; therefore, I look on you with love.

- My gifts to my brother heal us or condemn us. I choose to be a healer.

- I bless you wherever you are. May you be forever happy and free.

- I love you and I release you to follow God's will for you.

- I am willing to know the light in you, to believe in your process, to trust in God working through you.

- I will assist you in whatever way you ask. I release my investment in how you live your life.

- I see my brother (partner), happy, healed and whole.

- The more I bless you, the more I am blessed.

- We are One in the love we freely share.

Renewal and Remembrance

"Grant me Divine Serenity

To accept the things I cannot change,

The courage to change the things I can,

And the wisdom to know the difference."

- The Spirit of God flows through me, purifying and healing, bringing peace, health and harmony to my body, mind and soul.

- I am revitalized and renewed.

- I am beautiful, peaceful and poised.

- I am eternally youthful.

- I am buoyant, happy and free.

- I shall arise in the morning filled with energy, radiance and the power to accomplish whatever I am called to do.

- I am a perfect child of God.

- I am letting the mind of God express life and wholeness through me now.

- I am whole, happy and free.

- My mind, body and affairs are now in Divine order.

- I am healed. Praise God! I am healed.

- I am sustained by the Love of God.

- I am empowered by the Peace of God.

- I surrender only to God's love and God's power and God's peace.

- I dedicate this day to the highest and best in me.

Trust and Faith

- I trust my Self.

- I have faith in God.

- I trust in my life process.

- I trust in the perfection of others' life journeys and the choices they make.

- I believe that God is working through me in all ways.

- I have faith in my life journey.

  I let go of demanding that life be different than it is.

  My life is perfect now.

- I stay connected with the Inner Source.

- I can easily, quickly and safely do anything I want to do.

- I trust my Self, appreciate my Self and support my Self.

- God, I open my mind and my heart to Your Will for me.

- I put God first in my life.

- I am faithful to God. and Goodness.

- I shall be all that I am, letting go of anger, fear, guilt and pain.

- Being true to my Self is following the Highest Good in me.

- I let God lead the way.

- Being true is honoring who I am, my God-given gifts and my purpose here.

- I am willing to be true to my Self.

Healing and Clearing The Past

Forgiveness is an eraser filled with Love.

- All that has offended me, I forgive. Whatever I think has made me bitter, resentful, unhappy, I forgive. Within and without, I forgive. Whatever I have mistakenly judged, I forgive.

- I forgive positively everyone. I am free and they are free.

- Forgiveness is cleansing and clearing away the past. Forgiveness is selective remembering - remembering only what is beautiful, good and wholly loving. To be healthy and happy, I forgive.

- I am a forgiving being, and forgiveness comes naturally to me.

- Forgiveness frees us All. Therefore, I choose to forgive freely.

- Forgiving is fun, safe and easy.

- I fully and freely forgive anyone or anything that I have judged or feared in my past or present.

- I forgive you and I release you from my judgment.

- I am now forgiven by everything and everyone from the past.

- I am now forgiven by everything and everyone in the present.

- I am willing to forgive me for imagining separation from God.

- I love the light and life in me now.

- The more I forgive myself, the more I forgive others.

* The more I forgive myself, the more others forgive themselves.

• The more I forgive myself, the more others forgive me.

Use of Denial

You inflict dis-ease (a state of inner conflict) upon yourself by your fears, resentments, hates and beliefs in evil (error). Evil is any thought that is in opposition to eternal life and love.

Remember:

What you give attention to expands.

Denial is the first law of healing. "No, I do not accept this appearance as necessary or lasting in my life." There is no unhappiness in God. There need be no unhappiness in any of His creations.

Don't believe anything anyone tells you about your health, unless they tell you that you are well and whole. If they try to tell you anything else, refuse to listen and refuse to believe it.

- I deny fear. It is not real and has no power.
- I refuse to interfere with God's perfect plan.
- The process of life is unfolding in me now.
- There is no harm.
- The world and everyone in it wishes me well-being and happiness.
- There is nothing to fear.
- There is no power to hurt or be hurt in this situation.
- I believe no false beliefs. God is with me; I cannot be deceived.

Gratitude

- I fully and completely acknowledge and honor my being.
- I am grateful to God.
- I am grateful to myself for my willingness to play my part in life.
- I thank others for their integrity in choosing what is truly best for them.
- I thank You, God, for Your gifts to me.
- I value everyone's uniqueness.
- I look for good, then I praise it.
- I look for God, then I praise Him.
- I know everything works together for good.
- The more I appreciate what I give, the more I have.
- The more I appreciate what I have, the more I give.

Release • Letting Go • Detachment • Freedom

Through speaking words of release, our problems are freed to work out in whatever way is best. People naturally do the "right" thing when they are emotionally free to do so.

- I fully and freely release you. I loose you and let you go.
- All that has happened between us is now released.
- I free you to your Highest Good.
- The good of one is the good of all.
- I place this entire situation in God's hands and release it to His perfect solution.
- I release my family and friends to their own highest good.
- As I release you to your good, so I am released to mine.
- I now release all attachment to what I want.
- All Good is mine now.
- I release all secrets, withholds, uncertainty and resistance.
- There is nothing to fear.
- I now let go of fear and live with love.
- I release all obstacles to my health, happiness and freedom.
- I surrender to God and offer up my fearfulness.
- I release all obstacles to peace of mind and inner joy.
- Forgiveness is my function here.
- Letting go is fun, safe and easy.
- I can suffer no harm.

- I now release past judgments easily.

- The past no longer runs my thoughts, emotions or behavior.

- I welcome the opportunity to be free of all negativity, separation, guilt and pain.

- I choose release now.

- I let go of the past and experience being fully alive.

- I release the past and experience exactly who I am.

- I let go of all expectations and recognize everything is in perfect order.

- I release all that keeps me away from perfect joy.

I Am

Through right use of your "I AM" power, you will find yourself filled with the creative power of the universe, through which all things are possible.

- I am part of everything; I am perfect and whole.

- I am pure, simple and honest.

- I am evolving though the process of life, and I enjoy it.

- I am a radiant Child of God.

- I am sufficient and I am satisfied.

- I am a blessing.

- I am a channel for Spirit.

- I am a joy and delight for all to behold.

- I am the light of the world.

- I am my Self. I am whole and complete.

- God is love, therefore so am I.

- My direction is loving and clear.

- I am peace, joy and life.

- I am one with God and His Goodness.

- Praise God! I am healed.

- I am the radiant Child of God.

- I am the prosperous Child of God.

- I am the happy Child of God.

- I am the healthy Child of God.

- I am the illumined Child of God.

- I am the successful Child of God.

- I am loveable and capable.

- I am pleasing to myself in the presence of others.

- I am the loved and beloved Child of God.

- I am part of the creative power of the universe through which all things are possible.

- I am rich, well, happy and my affairs are now in Divine order.

- I am responsible for my own happiness.

- The Peace of God is shining in me now.

- I am blessed; therefore, I freely bless all.

- Everyday I am more and more open to All Good.

- I am alive, alert and enthusiastic.

- I am true to what is best for me.

- I am always in the right place at the right time doing the right thing.

- I am naturally pleasing in my innocent joy and love.

- I am limitless.

- I am free.

- I am truly as God created me.

- I serve only God and His purpose.

- I am here only for healing.

- I am filled with delight and I enjoy my life.

- I am here, wholly loveable and wholly loving.

- I am a beautiful, giving Child of God.

Healing

Healing occurs when even one of us releases all that was in the past with forgiveness and looks again with eyes filled with the vision of wholeness and holiness.

- I behold the Christ in you, and I am renewed in Faith.
- I am One with the Goodness, Beauty and Holiness which I see now in you.
- I praise God for the light within you.
- I look upon God's healing peace within your heart and see the holiness within you now.
- I am now allowing the Christ Mind to think through me.
- I see perfection and wholeness shining in you now.
- I see you healed and whole.
- When we are healed, we are not healed alone.
- Freedom is real and heaven is home.
- When the mind is healed, the body is seen as a temporary vehicle.
- I trust always in wholeness and holiness no matter appearances.

Vision

Hold the thought of what you would see, for thought is energy, and energy creates. Therefore, I create with my thoughts.

- I see my Self, perfect and whole, a pure expression of God, a light, innocent child.

- I experience Heaven here now.

- I see my own wholeness and the wholeness in All.

- God is the light in which I see.

- God is the mind with which I think.

- God is the love in which I forgive.

- God is the strength in which I trust.

- In God, there is nothing to fear.

- I see meaning in life and life has meaning.

- I see value in being and experience our worth.

- I see joy in giving and giving is joyful.

- What I believe, I experience.

- I see you free and happy and at peace.

- Having what I want will bring peace and love to everyone.

- I see a world of joy, a world of laughter, a world of love, a world of light and beauty and peace.

- I see a world with no money; everyone shares All with All; everyone freely gives what they love to give.

- I see everyone supporting each other with blessing, help and positive regard.

- I behold the Christ in you, and I am renewed in faith.

Health and Body

To picture health is one of the quickest roads to healing. To allow the body to heal, one must "image" or conceive it.

- Every day, in every way, I am getting better and better.

- I am healthy, vibrant, energized and revitalized by doing exactly what I choose to do.

- My mind infuses my body with loving thoughts of life, energy and health.

- I deserve to care for my health and my body.

- I eat exactly what is best for me.

- I rest and relax to maintain and enhance my perfect health and happiness.

- My mind is healthy; therefore, my body is healthy.

- I now breathe freely and easily.

- Breathing is fun.

- Every breath I breathe gives me life energy and health.

- My body is warm and yielding, fluid and healthy, graceful and healing, receptive and welcoming, powerful and willing to serve.

- My body and mind are healthy.

- I recognize my willingness to heal and be healed.

- Joy is health; I choose to enjoy everything in life.

- I keep myself physically healthy and receptive to more fun, fellowship and aliveness.

- My mind and my body are alive, alert and enthusiastic.

Commitment

- I set aside my littleness and follow God's Will for me.

- I commit my Self to following my Father's Will for me 100%. This is my life, the way I have freely and consciously chosen.

- I commit to the creation of unity, harmony, healing and abundance for all mankind.

- I commit to no secrets and no withholds.

- I 100% commit to happiness, aliveness and freedom.

- I am committed to unconditionally loving humanity.

- I am the Way, the Truth and the Life.

- I want peace; therefore, I see, live and speak nothing else.

- I think only thoughts I hold with God.

Parents

- Dad / Mom, I love you and I release you to be you. You are good, as am I, perfect and whole.

- I forgive you, (Dad/Mom) for:

  ignoring me.

  arguing with me.

  putting me down.

  disappointing me.

  being jealous of me.

  being afraid of me.

- I forgive you, (Dad/Mom) for being loving and affectionate with everyone else more easily than with me.

- With you, (Dad/Mom), I forgive myself for:

  limiting myself.

  not fully expressing my Self.

  being afraid to love and accept you.

  being disappointed in you.

  feeling hurt and left out.

  being afraid to be my Self.

  being afraid to express my Self.

  withholding affection from you.

- I forgive you (Dad/Mom), for not seeing me truly.

- I forgive you (Dad/Mom), for your limited and false beliefs about yourself and about me.

- I forgive you (Dad/Mom), for projecting your pain and judgment onto me.

- I forgive you (Dad/Mom), for not recognizing your own wholeness, goodness and beauty.

- I no longer need your approval (Dad/Mom); I now approve of my Self.

- I now release all that I thought was done to me.

- I forgive myself for my misperceptions.

- I am now willing to see clearly that all lack of love is a call for love.

- I forgive you (Dad/Mom), for not knowing any better.

- I forgive you (Dad/Mom), for feeling guilty about how you loved me.

- I forgive you (Dad/Mom) for not spending enough time with me.

- I release my parents. I am now true to my Self.

- I forgive myself for believing you hurt me.

- I forgive myself for believing I deserved what you told me.

- I forgive myself for forgetting what is true for me about me.

- I forgive myself for believing you knew the Truth about me.

- I forgive myself for giving you power over me.

- I forgive myself for letting you limit me.

- I now set myself free to see you as temporary guardians, doing the best you knew.

Life

- Life is child's play, a Divine comedy. I no longer choose to play my part seriously for I know we are all learning.

- When I know I am whole and perfect, I will create only what is good, beautiful and holy.

- The more I support my own happiness, the more I support others' happiness.

- I now love others as I prefer to be loved by them.

- The more freely I love, the more fully I am loved.

- The more I love myself, the more I love others.

- The more I love myself, the more others love me.

- The more I love myself, the more others love themselves.

- Life is for loving and learning. I delight in life.

- I love life and life loves me.

- The Universe supports me, and affirms my thoughts.

- Today is the first day of the rest of my life.

- I relax and enjoy what God has given.

- In my freedom from want, I am generous and open and honest.

- In my freedom, I am whole and good and happy.

- In my freedom from duty, I am trusting, patient and tolerant.

- The more I am free, the more I am responsive to everyone and every situation.

- In freedom, I find God.

- God loves me and provides for my every need.

- I forgive myself for getting lost in fear and guilt.

- I am free to love you and me right now.
- Being free to love brings light and joy.
- I want only truth; therefore, I see nothing else.

Prosperity and Success

Prosperity is the product of love in action.

To receive more, be willing to give more of your Self.

- The more successful I am, the more others are successful.
- I am willing to let every need be provided.
- I express gratitude to everyone who gives me money.
- The more gratitude I experience (give), the more prosperity and success I have.
- I am successful and prosperous.
- I am open to receive great prosperity now.
- I release my fears and judgments of being rich.
- I know the more I give, the more I have.
- The more prosperity and success I have, the more fully I live.
- The more prosperity and success I have, the more freely I love.
- The more prosperity and success I have, the more I give.
- I am good; therefore, I attract only good.
- People love to pay me for doing what I love.
- I am willing to receive an abundance of success, financial prosperity and self-fulfillment in my work.
- In my prosperity, I am generous and honest.
- God wants me to have my Highest Good.
- Being successful is good for everyone.
- I can now have everything I truly want.
- No one and nothing limits me.

- I have an abundance of power and peace.

- Nothing holds me back.

- Every limiting thought I correct easily and quickly.

- The more I know I am One with Him, the more I am willing to experience all abundance.

- I claim my good now.

- My consciousness increases and expands the good I see, the good I affirm, the good that I am.

- My life is rich with goodness, beauty and wholeness.

- I see it, I affirm it, and I appreciate it.

- I bless money and use it for good.

- I always have an unlimited supply of money.

- Money comes to me easily.

- Money works for me.

- I pay all debts easily and quickly with joy.

- The more I spend, the more I have.

- The more I appreciate myself, the more others appreciate me.

- The more I appreciate others, the more others appreciate themselves.

- I am willing to be what I want to be.

- I am willing to do what I want to do.

- I am willing to have what I want to have.

- I am willing to have an abundant life.

- I am now surrounded with happy, grateful people.

Willingness

- I am willing to be an enlightened, healing being.

- I am willing to be a blessing to everyone who comes into my presence or who thinks of me.

- I am willing to be a peaceful channel for God's goodness and mercy.

- I am willing to lose, to fail, to let go, to stretch and to be.

- I am willing to take a stand.

- I am willing to confront differences.

- I am willing to be true to my highest values.

- I am willing to be and do whatever serves the good of the whole.

- I am willing to be all I am, all of the time, in the presence of all.

- I am willing to be my own best friend.

- I am willing to be open, intuitive, creative and expansive.

- I am willing to be alive and vital in every beautiful moment.

- I am willing to experience miracles all day.

- I am willing to love and appreciate my Self for each learning experience, each mistake corrected and each gift I share with others.

- I am now willing to say "No" when it is not in my best interest.

- I am willing to serve myself with joy; there is no greater service.

- I am willing to spread my light and offer joy.

Knowledge

I am clearly a learner in life, so I must focus on the teachings first. When I forget the Truth, I become lost. When I recognize I am lost, I ask to be found, to right my path.

- I am satisfied not knowing anything.
- I know my True identity and I am grateful.
- I know Truth and I trust it.
- I share Truth with lightness and laughter.
- I trust I am good.
- I know I am good.
- I was born good and will always be good.
- No matter what changes in the world, peace and love and Good are constant in me.

Truth

- I know the Truth is simple, easy, safe and lasting.
- I know that to attack is to fear being attacked.
- I know satisfaction in experiencing completion.
- I know that I reap what I sow.
- I know security in my willingness to take risks.
- I know mistakes are opportunities for learning and healing.
- I know that to be a true teacher, I am constantly learning.
- I know that to serve is to forgive, to pass no judgment and to see sinlessness in my brothers and sisters.
- Everything always works more exquisitely than I can plan.
- I give everything I see all the meaning it has for me.
- Through deliberate constructive use of my imagination, I produce wonderful changes in my body.
- God works through all things.
- What I resist, persists.
- What I give energy to (pay attention to), expands.
- I know happiness in celebrating every moment of my life.
- I know sacrifice comes only from denying my inner voice.
- Quieting my mind promotes directed action.
- My security and freedom are found within.
- In balance, I am at peace.
- I know my best in trusting every moment.
- I need do nothing. My power is of God.
- God is with me. I share His love.

- I know everything is on purpose.
- God is energy, life force, the Creator of all being. I now choose what I do with my energy.
- I know to share only Truth is to learn perfectly.
- Others treat me as I treat myself.
- I now treat my Self well.
- Playing serves everyone.

Acceptance and Forgiveness

- I accept failure and success.

- I no longer fear being fearful.

- I forgive my judgments of others.

- I forgive myself for finding fault with you and your process.

- I forgive myself for efforting to be free of mistakes.

- Mistakes give me the opportunity for growth.

- I forgive myself for sacrificing.

- I forgive myself for denying myself and limiting myself.

- I wholly accept my Holiness as a beloved Child of God.

- I freely forgive you.

- I freely let you go.

- I let go all false concepts about you.

- I see only your wholeness and perfection.

- I forgive myself for limiting myself and my work.

- I forgive all who have offended me.

- I accept my part in God's plan for salvation.

- I know my part in God's plan is one of perfect peace and happiness.

- I accept the way it is for me right now.

Love

- Only love can lead the way.

- Only love heals.

- Only love can teach.

- Love is being true to my Self. I am now true to my Self.

- I now love my True Self first.

- I love my purpose in life and my unique gifts.

- It is my joy to share my life and my unique gifts.

- I know my love is essential to the world.

- I am here to be love everywhere with everyone.

- I am the love of God personified.

- I know people give and receive love easily.

- I deserve to be loved.

- I am willing to know and love my Self as I really am.

- There is nothing to do except be the love that I am.

- I am a gift to the world.

- I came to offer love to the world.

- I am love, pure, good and whole.

- I am willing to be wholly loved and guided today.

Relationships

- I release you to your Highest Good.

- I love you and I give you peace.

- God, in His infinite wisdom, has sent you to me that I might learn the true meaning of Divine Love.

- I am willing to love you without regard for what the body is or for what the body does.

- I release any desire to control your life.

- I open to a whole, completely healing, freeing, Eternal relationship - beyond all time and space - given to God for His Plan and His Purpose.

- Let our function together be shown to us.

- I am willing to love you beyond all condition; to love even as God loves.

- I release all resentment, guilt and fear, and open fully to know only God's love.

- I know God is working through us now and I am glad.

- I am willing to be a blessing to you in our life together.

- I see you as a gift to me and I am grateful.

- My partner and I trust and support each other.

- The more I freely give to my partner, the happier he is and the more our love grows.

- I now want only peace and happiness for my partner.

- You are pleasing to me as you are.

- My love is healthy, lasting and unconditional.

- I am highly pleasing to myself in my loved one's presence.

- Spirit is the source of our commitment to one another.

- We wholly support each other's growth and total acceptance of the guidance of Spirit.

- I love and accept you as you are, and you encourage me to grow in loving my Self more completely.

- I open in innocence and in love.

- I am willing to receive an abundance of success, prosperity and happiness in my relationship.

- I make myself happy and give others the space in which to create their own happiness and fulfillment.

- Nothing you can do or say can hurt me. I am loved, loveable and loving.

- I now experience limitless love and forgiveness flowing between us.

I Am All That I Am
I Love All That I Am

- I now live a life of love.

- I now live my life at peace.

- I am in love with all.

- I bring forgiveness and joy.

- I share God's gifts to me.

- My partner and I walk hand in hand together with God.

- I am happy.

- I am alive fully every moment.

- I live eternally.

- I am free.

- I easily correct all mistakes.

- I see only the good, beautiful and whole.

- I sing and dance and have fun.

- I put God first in my life.

- I am faithful to God.

- I share my love for God and my joy for life.

- I have an all-inclusive loving, healing, happy family.

- I fully support my own process.

- I trust my journey.

- I surrender all hesitation, uncertainty and self-blame.

- I live in God's glorious playground.

- I love, laugh and learn from every experience.

- I share and contribute what I am learning.
- I am always cared for and loved.
- I am unique.
- I am where I want to be.
- I need do nothing.
- I am ready.
- My mind is clear.
- I am peaceful.
- I am willing to meditate regularly.
- I let love lead the way.
- The more content and happy I am, the more love is shared.

Guilt and Forgiveness

If you feel guilty, you will tend to do what is bad for you, what brings you pain and more guilt. If you are guiltless, you will choose to do your Father's Will, what is truly for the Good of All.

- I forgive them for they know not what they do.
* I forgive them for fearing and judging me.
- I forgive myself for taking on others' fear.
- I now take in only love and share that love freely.
- I forgive myself

    for withholding love.

    for limiting my Self.

    for feeling guilty.

    for being afraid.

    for my judgments.

    for rejecting life.

    for denying myself.

    for forgetting myself.

Let's Wake Up Smiling
And Use Our Affirmations

Be Aware

See what you have chosen, your learning perceptions, your judgments, your fears, your shadowy limitations and illusions of lack.

Acknowledge

Express what you want to see differently, where you want transformation and healing of your perceptions.

Allow

Let go of your mistaken perceptions and faulty thinking. Release the illusion and be open for Truth, which will come to you as you use your affirmations.

Affirm

State clearly the choice to know only Truth, see only Light, and experience Wholeness, Goodness and Beauty. Choose for the highest and best in your life, for such is God's Will.

Accept

All good is our Divine Right, so honor and respect what you truly deserve.

Appreciate

Give joyful thanks for all good and be generous in your gifts to the Source of All Good.

To awaken is to forgive the world and heal the past.

Enlightenment is seeing what is good and beautiful and holy.

Affirmations For Conscious Healing

- Letting go is fun, safe and easy.
- I now easily bless and release all that no longer serves me.
- I forgive with ease and let go with gratitude.
- Everyone and everything is either giving love or calling for Love.
- I am a Love giver.
- The more I give Love, the more I have the Love I want.
- Light, light, I want more light.
- I choose to live with joy and give with gratitude.
- I love my life and it loves me.
- I have what I want and share the best I have.
- Life works for me.
- I am the chooser, never a loser.
- Everything always works more exquisitely than I can plan.
- I trust in my inner knowing, always gentle, loving and true.
- I let go of expectations, evaluations and disappointments.
- I am creating a world of healing and love one person at a time.
- The more I love and respect myself, the more others love and respect me.
- The more I love and respect myself, the more I love and respect others.
- The more I love and respect myself, the more others love and respect themselves.
- I am clear, focused and committed.

- I consciously communicate exactly what I want.
- I give myself the very best and all are blessed.
- I am present, peaceful, awake and aware.
- I share only the highest Truth I know and then I let go.
- My happiness is contagious.
- I replace all worry, fear and doubt with trust, freedom and blessing.
- Peace and love and joy heal us All.
- My body is a vehicle for learning only Love is Real.

Loving Reminder Affirmations

I am radiant with confidence and the Love of God.

Every thought, word and deed teaches everyone.

I choose to think, speak and act with loving kindness.

I am a Loving Reminder.

I am here to be love, to express love, to give and receive love.

I am available with Love and Spirit for those who seek my help and counsel.

My relationships are honest, respectful and trusting.

I am a teacher of God.

Every thought, word and action is inspired and inspiring.

I am utilized by Spirit to create all that is Good, Beautiful and Holy.

I am willing to be a shining star for God.

I respect who I am.

I love my life.

I believe in my God-given gifts.

I no longer take myself for granted.

I am guided to live joyfully and give abundantly.

I love living in clean, beautiful, harmonious spaces, at home and when I travel, where goodness and wholeness are obvious.

I treat myself with dignity, respect and appreciation.

I have no worries or concerns.

God provides perfectly for my needs.

I am grateful those who serve me are honest, conscious and caring.

I am inspired, focused and Spirit-guided in All I do.

I deserve a beautiful, fulfilling and prosperous life rich with opportunity, adventure, creativity and friendship.

I am surrounded by people who value, trust and support me.

My life works because I do my spiritual work.

Love is letting go of fear.

Only Love is real. Everything else is made up.

My direction is freedom and my goal is the Peace of God.

We are all created by Love, as Love, for the purpose of Loving.

I see more clearly. I love more purely. I follow God more nearly. Day by day.

Life is for Giving. I am the Gift.

Seek first for Good. Everything else follows.

Life is Good and getting better.

I easily and quickly release all negativity and trust only in Good.

My mind automatically erases everything that is not wholly True and wholly Loving.

God grant me the courage to change the things I can;
The patience to accept the things I cannot change;
The wisdom to know the difference;
And the willingness to see choices where I thought there were none.

Every little cell in my body is happy. Every little cell in my body is whole

Every step I take is Holy Ground.
Every word I speak is True. Every song I sing of Holiness is giving Praise to You.

The Light of God surrounds me.
The Love of God enfolds me.
The Power of God directs me.
The Presence of God watches over me.
Wherever I am, God is. And all is well.

I enjoy eating beautiful, nutritious, lovingly prepared meals, which revitalize my perfectly healthy and youthful body.

My spiritual and worldly resources perfectly support my magnanimous philosophy and creative service for the Good of All.

I totally appreciate Who I Am, How I Live and All I Give.

I forgive everything and everyone everyday, including myself.

Give Your Self To Love And Love Will Give To You.

I rest in the Love of God as I am always loving.

Letting go is fun, safe and easy.

As I easily release my attachments, life is fun, safe and easy.

I am a whole and powerful Child of God.

I think, speak and live in God. My life is an activity of Spirit.

Making mistakes is a wonderful learning opportunity.

I celebrate all I am learning.

I easily forgive the past and trust the future, as I live a Spirit-guided life.

My mind and body are easily guided by Spirit.

I am an instrument of Love Itself.

Everything is in Divine Order.

It may not be comfortable, yet it is in Divine Order.

I am enough.

I relax and trust Spirit is perfectly working in my life.

I now attract the perfect people and circumstances to create an abundant life of good works and service.

I am a Spiritual Being having a physical world experience.

To know me is to love me.

The more I love and respect my Self, the more others love and respect me.

I forgive myself for withholding love and joy.

I give All to All for the blessing of All.

Life can be fun, safe and easy.

We're the same, you and I. We're in this together.

My forgiveness and gratitude heal all things.

I live in trust, knowing that all my needs are perfectly provided for.

I am what I choose to be; I now choose what is best for me.

I love my Self well; therefore I always have an abundance of Love to give.

The only mistake we ever make is when we forget to love.

I am now surrounded by supportive, inspired, prosperous people who love what they do and do what they love.

I dedicate this day to the highest and best in me.

Everything works more exquisitely than I can plan.

I have faith in my life journey.

I let go of demanding that life be different than it is.

I am whole and happy and free.

I am highly pleasing to myself in the presence of everyone.

I am willing to be my True Self.

Forgiveness frees everyone; I choose to forgive freely.

I choose to see the Love which transcends all anger and dissolves all fear.

I release all obstacles to health, happiness and freedom.

I see my own Wholeness and the Wholeness in everyone.

I want only Truth; therefore, I see nothing else.

My mind is healthy; therefore, my body is healthy.
Every day, in every way, I am getting better and better.

I want peace; therefore I see, live and speak only peace.

The more I support my own happiness, the more I support others' happiness.

When I know I am whole and perfect, I create only what is good, beautiful & holy.

I am willing to be all that I want to be.

I love life and life loves me.

I am good; therefore I attract only good.

I am willing to experience miracles all day, every day.

I can now have everything I truly want, which serves my Highest Good.

No one and nothing limits me.

I know Truth and I trust it.

I share Truth with lightness and laughter.

My mind and body are alive, alert and enthusiastic.

I am willing to be and do whatever serves the Good All.

I know happiness in celebrating every moment of my life.

Joy is health; I choose to enjoy everything in life.

God is with me every moment of the day.

God is with me every step of the way.

I recognize all Holy Ones as messengers of Divine Love and Divine Truth.

I am willing to be true to my highest values.

With a clear mind I can see what is Real.

I now eat and drink only what supports my whole life health.

I am free of all seeming tribulation and lack.

I live in freedom and abundance everyday.

God is All I know.
God is where I go.
God is how I show
The Love You give to me.

We are calling forth the Light with every prayer of gratitude and every song of praise.

No matter what changes in the world, peace and love are constant in me.

Life is for loving and learning and letting go.

In freedom, I find God.

God loves me and provides for my every need.

I commit to the creation of unity, harmony, healing and abundance for all mankind.

The Universe supports me and affirms my thoughts.

I forgive myself for getting lost in fear and guilt.

I am committed to unconditionally loving humanity.

In my freedom from want, I am generous and open and honest.

I want only Truth; therefore, I see nothing else.

I want peace; therefore, I see, live and speak nothing else.

I now accept only those thoughts and beliefs which add to my life.

Every breath I breathe gives me life energy, health and peace of mind.

The more I heal my Self, the more humanity is healed.

I am healthy, vibrant, energized and revitalized by doing exactly what I choose to do.

I recognize and respect my willingness to heal and be healed.

I keep myself physically healthy and receptive to more fun, fellowship and aliveness.

I now breathe freely and easily.

Joy is health. I choose to enjoy everything in life.

I like my Real Self. I encourage my Essence.

I trust choices made in Love for the sake of Love.

I am willing to let every need be perfectly provided.

I have an abundance of power, prosperity and peace.

I freely speak the Truth, and trust it serves all.

I know the more I give, the more I have.

Nothing holds me back.

I meet every fear with Love, and every fear resolves and dissolves.

No one and nothing limits me.

I claim My Good now.

My life is rich with goodness, beauty and wholeness.

I see it, I affirm it and I appreciate it.

I choose what I want to see; I see Holiness and Truth.

What is best for me is best for others.

I now choose to play the game of life to a joyous win for all.

I do what brings me joy and feel good about it.

I choose to have life and have it more and more abundantly.

I know what is right and good for me.

Everything I want, I have.

I choose only that which is Best for me.

I know what is right and good for me.

I choose peace for it brings me rest and renewal.

I am now surrounded by happy, grateful people.

I am willing to take a stand for the Highest Truth.

I am willing to be open, intuitive, creative and expansive.

I want all these things I have affirmed, or something better.

I am willing to be and do whatever serves the Good of the Whole.

I now experience miracles all day.

I am willing to be a blessing to everyone who comes into my presence or who thinks of me.

I am willing to be All I Am, all of the time, in the presence of all.

I free myself and you of all past judgments, pain and fear.

I set us all free to be.

I bless you wherever you are.

May you be forever happy and free.

I see my brothers happy, healed and whole.

To serve is to forgive, to pass no judgment and to see sinlessness in my brothers and sisters.

I love you and I release you to follow God's Will for you.

The more I bless, the more I am blessed.

Everything always works more exquisitely than I can plan.

I am willing to know the Light in you, to believe in your process, to trust in God working through you.

I am willing to shine my Light and share my Joy.

God works through all things.

What I resist persists.

What I give energy to (pay attention to) expands.

I now communicate fully and freely I am willing to be honest and open.

Others treat me as I treat myself. I now treat my Self well.

I am willing to be a channel for good news and Love.

I am willing to see the Love which transcends all fear.

I know I am good. I was born good and will always be good.

I now communicate my thoughts and feelings with joy, ease and safety.

Quieting my mind promotes directed action.

No matter what changes in the world, peace and love are constant in me.

I am revitalized and renewed.

I dedicate this day to the Highest and Best in me.

I forgive myself for limiting myself and my work.

My mind, body and affairs are now in Divine Order.

I forgive myself for sacrificing.

I forgive myself for denying myself and limiting myself.

I know that God is working through me in all ways.

I am healed. Praise God! I am healed.

I let go all false concepts about you. I see only your wholeness and perfection.

I trust my Self, appreciate my Self and support my Self.

I have faith in my life journey.

I let go of demanding that life be different than it is.

My life is perfect now.

I trust my Self, appreciate my Self and support my Self.

I am willing to be true to my Self.

I know my love is essential to the world.

I put God and Good first in my life.

Nothing you can do or say can hurt me.

I am loved, loveable and loving.

I am here to be Love, everywhere with everyone.

I let Love lead the way.

I love my purpose in life and my unique gifts.

It is my joy to share my life and my unique gifts.

I am willing to be wholly loved and guided today.

I forgive positively everyone.

I am free and they are free.

I forgive myself for taking on others' fear.

I free you to your Highest Good.

I am a forgiving being.

Forgiveness comes naturally to me.

I deny fear; It is not real and has no power.

As I release you to your good, so I am released to mine.

I am now forgiven by everything and everyone of the past, present and future.

I believe no false beliefs. God is with me. I cannot be deceived.

I release all secrets, withholds, uncertainty and resistance.

There is nothing to fear.

I release all obstacles to my health, happiness and freedom.

As I let go of all expectations, I recognize everything is in perfect order.

I am a blessing.

I am a channel for Spirit.

Forgiveness is my function here.

Letting go is fun, safe and easy.

The more I appreciate what I give, the more I have.
The more I appreciate what I have, the more I give.

I am a joy and delight for all to behold.

I am the Light of the World.

I welcome the opportunity to be free of all negativity, separation, guilt and pain. I choose release now.

I am sufficient and I am satisfied.

God is Love, therefore so am I.

I am loveable and capable.

I am highly pleasing to myself in the presence of others.

God is the Light in which I see.
God is the Mind with which I think.
God is the Love in which I forgive.
God is the Strength in which I trust.
In God, there is nothing to fear.

I delight in being lovingly touched and blessed physically, emotionally, mentally, financially, and spiritually.

I am blessed, therefore I freely bless all.

We are loved.
We are blessed.
Because we are Divine.

I create my life for the extension of Love and expression of Self and Love for God.

I am limitless. I am free. I am as God created me.

I ask for help when I have need. I let go and trust God.

I awaken others to Spirit with my Presence, my Vision and my Voice.

I rest in God and trust all is in Divine Order no matter the appearance.

I take exquisite care of and enjoy the gift of the life I am given every day.

I live, work and play with happy, conscious, creative and generous people—loving, laughing, learning and letting go as we live in Joy together.

I am alive with enthusiastic possibility, joyful creativity and confident expression.

To love is the freedom to do what you enjoy.

I love living in a happy and grateful world.

I treat all Beings with love and respect.

My body works for me, as I fully appreciate it.

I love who I am, all that I do and how I am loved and supported.

I enjoy using my beautiful, energetic body only for loving purposes and maintaining perfect health.

I am totally supported by my thoughts, words and activities and by my world in having what I really want, in being All I can be, and in giving freely All I Am.

To be in equal partnership is to fully play our part in God's plan.

All my relationships are harmonious, respectful and loving.

I live, play and work with elegant ease and a light-hearted spontaneity.

I know who I Am and I love being me.

I refuse to allow limitations, lack and littleness to detour or delay me.

I am truly blessed.

I give thanks for my unlimited life of creativity and service.

I am filled with possibility thinking and thoroughly enjoy the abundant fruits of my success.

More Affirmations for You

You Are Responsible for Your Own Happiness

I am willing to be totally responsible for my own happiness.

I love myself and choose to be happy.

I now give and receive All Good and Only Good.

Life Is Not About Being Perfect!

I am always in the right place, doing the right thing, for the right reasons.

Stop Fighting and Start Listening

I quickly forgive my anger, hurt and resentment.

I release all pettiness, resistance and need to be right.

I listen with patience, respect and acceptance.

I prefer to be happy and live in harmony.

Keep Your Vision in Mind

Life works for me, because I am grateful for the Life I have.

Everything works together for Good, because everything is in my best interests.

I now gratefully seek and find the gift and blessing in every experience.

Self-Remembering

I love, trust and respect my Self.

I see and know my True and Authentic Self.

I am free and unlimited.

Addictions and Self-Discipline

I easily and quickly let go of the limiting and distracting habits and addictions in my life.

I love and respect myself and my healthy choices.

I now choose what is best for me.

Life Happens!

Everything is in my own best interests.

I easily and quickly learn from everything.

I forgive and see things differently.

I am at peace, because I live in trust with the Good that always is.

Afraid to Love?

The more I Love, the healthier and happier I am.

Extending Love, loves me mightily.

Love is the way I live in freedom and trust.

I forgive my fear and let Love lead the way.

Kindness and Consideration

I choose the gentle path of kindness and consideration.

I am blessed with well-being, as I am kind to everyone.

Life is sweet, when I consider the well-being of others.

All is well, when I remember the kindness within me.

Rise Up or Sink Down?

I quickly release negativity, judgment and doubt.

I align my thoughts and words with the Highest Good.

I keep my most inspiring visions before me.

I trust in God and Good in all things.

Remember to Say "Good Bye"

I love you and release you to your Highest Good.

I am happy. I am free. I am complete.

I forgive everyone and everything all the time, including myself.

I complete every relationship with respect, honor and appreciation.

Who Is Leading You?

I follow the path of doing Good for myself and others.

I listen to the guide that lives in me and knows only the best I can be.

I trust Spirit within to inspire and guide my life.

Commit or Quit?

I always choose for the Highest Good of all.

My life works, because I do the work everyday.

I commit to the best and live in integrity with my commitments.

I easily and endlessly commit to what is Good.

I do not quit on myself or others.

Trust and Let Go of Control

I forgive the past and trust in the Presence of Goodness and Love.

I release and let go of you: I let Spirit run your life.

I choose for love, freedom and trust for us all.

I release you and all to our highest Good.

I affirm life, liberty and the pursuit of happiness for one and all.

Integrity

I am loveable, capable and willing.

I see, know and love my Real Self.

I quickly and easily release all thoughts and feelings that limit me.

I give myself the freedom and trust, goodness and Love I deserve.

Want To Be Happy?

I choose to be happy with myself and my world.

The more I choose happiness, the more I feel loved and loving.

I would rather be happy, than try to be right.

Life works for me when I am happy with life.

Past, Present, Future

The past is gone: it has no power.

I place my future in the hands of God.

I live in the Power of Now.

I enjoy this moment for the gift it presents to me.

Serenity Prayer

I choose to accept life and respond with love.

I choose to change what I am able to change easily.

I choose to be wise and flexible in my choices.

I easily adapt to changing circumstances with ease and grace.

How Do You Love?

I love myself well, just as I am.

The more I love, accept and respect myself, the more I love, accept and respect others.

Self Love is the key to fully and freely loving others.

Trouble, Transition or Transformation

Everything happens more exquisitely than I can plan.

All things work together for Good.

I am alive, alert and enthusiastic.

Life works for me, because I do the work.

What You Believe Is How You Live

I choose what works for me.

What is best for me is best for others.

I know what I want and I go for it.

I live true to my beliefs and values.

Communication and Correspondence

Everything I think and say and do is teaching everyone in my world.

There are no secrets: we are connected all the time.

I am always loving you, as I love myself.

Giving is receiving: I receive everything as I have given.

What Do You Believe?

I love myself no matter what.

I treat myself with loving kindness.

I respond to my inner voice and intuition with respect.

I take full responsibility for the quality of my life.

Light Brings Awakening

I know who I am.

I remember my Holy Purpose.

I see myself whole, happy and good.

I give the best of me freely and easily to all.

Who Runs Your Life?

I know what I want and I go for it!

I love the choices I make.

Making mistakes is a great learning experience.

I easily forgive all mistakes and learn what works.

Letting go and moving on is fun, safe and easy.

Relationships Teach Us

I give and receive love and appreciation in all my relationships.

I treat everyone equally with respect and gratitude.

I forgive myself for any mistake I make and choose again for the best I know.

I easily release my judgments, fears and resentment and choose for loving kindness.

I treat others with the kindness and respect we all deserve.

Be Responsible for Yourself!

I forgive myself for blaming or playing victim.

I release all fear of being fully responsible.

Being responsible is fun, safe and easy for me.

I am willing to forgive and choose again.

I create my experience and enjoy learning from everything.

How Do I Do It?

I appreciate and freely share all the Good I have.

I trust the Good in me and all the Good I see.

Giving expands the Good I have and share.

I am Good and Good begets only Good.

Work More, Enjoy More

I do the work I enjoy and I enjoy the work I do.

Happy thoughts create happy work; happy work creates happy lives.

I love clearing away everything that is negative and unloving.

Life works for me because I do the work.

I receive fully from everything I give freely.

Great Relationships Begin with You

All good relationships begin with Me.

I am willing to be the One to remember Love.

I am willing to let go of trying to get you to be the One.

I know when I am willing, everyone benefits.

Sacrifice Does Not Work!

I no longer dare to compare, evaluate and expect more.

I give my best with Joy.

I receive the Good I give with gratitude.

I appreciate unconditional giving and receiving.

I now give simply to enjoy freely giving.

Freedom

I am not my body; I am free.

I am not my emotions; I am free.

I am not my thoughts; I am free.

I am free to change my physical being, my feelings and my thoughts.

I choose to free my whole self to be the Love I am here to be.

I choose to be free and trust in the Love in me.

Levels of Love's Expression

Love is my natural state.

Where I am withholding Love, I forgive myself.

When we love, we are happy and at peace.

Love is trust and freedom.

I trust us to free ourselves to be the Love We Are.

Love reminds us that we are Love.

Thank You for Waiting

Anything I value is worth waiting for.

I value love and am patient in my loving.

I am patient, even with my impatience.

I am here to use the time I have to give all I have to give.

Sometimes We Are Mistaken!

I am willing to be wrong.

All mistakes are opportunities to forgive and learn.

I easily and quickly forgive all mistakes, yours, mine and ours.

I am willing to see things differently.

I trust all things work together for Good.

Do Your Spiritual Work!

I do everything I do with Love.

I know we are the same in Truth.

I enjoy and appreciate the unique parts we play.

I trust, respect and Love You, as I trust respect and Love Me.

Where Are You Going?

I am the One I seek to be.

I live my life in integrity.

I always listen to the voice within.

Vision...Purpose...Mission...Goals

I know Who I Am.

I know the calling of my heart.

I live my purpose and mission.

Goodness is my life and I serve it well.

I live what I value in every aspect of my life.

Healing

I am whole and complete; I am free.

I forgive my belief in sickness and death.

I trust in the perfect health and abundance in me.

I am not a body: I am free. I am as I was created to be.

What's Holding You Back?

I know what I want and I go for it.

I know who I really am and I live it.

I trust the Good in me and I give it.

I Am that I AM…..and so are You.

Can You Imagine?

I know who I am and I am true to myself.

No one and nothing can stop me from being me.

I love who I am and all that I give.

I enjoy my whole life and how I choose to live.

Life works for me, because I do the work.

What Do You Want?

I know what I want and I go for it.

I am filled with all I need to easily achieve what I desire.

I seek and speak only what is for the highest good of all.

I am Good and choose what expands the Good in me.

Heal the Past

As I heal, I reveal all the Good in me.

I let go of what was, in order to receive the Good in what is.

I see Who I AM, as I am willing to see Who You Really Are.

Give All to All

I naturally share the Good in me with all I see.

All I give with joy is returned to me in abundance.

I am creating an abundant world with abundant thoughts, words and deeds.

I am a rich woman in a rich world of Goodness, Beauty and Love.

I share what is real and eternal, the riches of Joy and Gratitude and Peace.

Relationships Are For Healing

I cannot see what I think cannot be.

I choose to see what I believe can be for me.

My mind now automatically erases everything that is not wholly true and loving.

I erase all fear and doubt and teach what love is all about.

I now relate to everyone with kindness and respect all the time.

Stop Blaming!

I no longer complain, criticize or blame myself or others.

I now affirm, accept and appreciate the Good in me and all.

I choose to forgive and release judgmental thoughts and words.

I trust we are all where we need to be to heal and learn and grow.

The more I free myself from negativity, the more I see Who I really Am.

Energy Creates More Energy

The more I love, the happier, healthier and more productive I am.

I am highly energized by everything I think, say and do.

I release all fear and relinquish all attack: I live at peace within myself.

Life works for me as I do the work.

Everything works together for good, when I remember this is my truth.

Light, Light, More Light

I am light in my thoughts, words and relationships.

I shine the light and clear all darkness, ignorance and fear.

I am filled with deLight as I share the happiness inside.

The more I forgive, the Lighter I Am.

It is the most natural thing in the world to be Light and give Love.

Are You Where You Want To Be?

I am here to be truly helpful.

My life supports me in living my purpose.

I love being fully alive and freely sharing my gifts.

I am here to relinquish all apparent blocks to Love.

It's All Good!

I now receive all Good and only Good.

I am open and willing to see the Good in everything.

I love my life and my life loves me.

I choose wisely what is for the highest Good of all.

Explore and Learn!

I am curious and full of wonder as I explore.

I love learning and exploring new ideas.

I enjoy the experiences I create and appreciate.

I forgive any mistakes or misperceptions.

What Are You Learning?

Love is the way to peace.

I quickly recognize, forgive and erase all blocks to Love.

It is safe, fun and easy to love, only Love.

All good comes from Loving, without condition or specialness.

Where Is Your Power?

I commit myself and my life to doing only Good.

I choose for what is a blessing to everyone.

I recognize and honor the power of contribution.

I communicate only the best I know.

Are You Loving You?

I love, trust, respect and appreciate myself.

I forgive myself for denying what is truly best for me.

Everything I give is given to myself.

I now receive all Good and give only Good to all.

I delight in the life I have created for myself.

What Will It Take for Us to Learn?

I forgive myself for acting opinionated and stuck.

Learning is fun, safe and easy.

Everything works together for Good.

Life teaches me with everything I experience.

I ingest the best and forget the rest.

Family Healing

Forgiveness sets me free.

I quickly and easily forgive all blocks to Love.

I extend peace, so that I may experience Peace.

I receive what I give with gratitude for the gift.

I know what I want and so it is what I give.

Life Works

I am awake and aware and create with wisdom and love.

My life works for me, because I do the work.

I create only Goodness, Wholeness and Love for All.

I use my thoughts, words and actions for Goodness Sake.

Life Is For Love

I am created by Love as Love for the purpose of Loving.

Love is my natural state.

My purpose here is to forgive all lack of Love.

I remember I am here for the purpose of seeing and being, having and giving only Love.

Are You Responsible?

I am willing to respond with Love.

I am willing to care for my whole Self so I am able to respond with Love.

I choose to be responsible for my self, my life and my relationships.

I forgive all mistakes and choose better ways to live.

Love Waits on Welcome

Today I affirm my whole Self in every way.

Today I demonstrate real authentic Love and respect for myself.

Today I teach others how to be responsible and respectful.

Today I live a life I am truly pleased by and proud of.

Today I genuinely Love me.

Do You Really Want to Have a Good Life?

I am Good. I do Good. I have Goodness in my life.

I happily work everyday to create and enjoy the life I have.

Life works for me, because I work for Good for me and all.

I trust the choices I make and appreciate all I am learning and remembering.

Forgiveness Works!

I forgive myself for hurting others with my judgments.

I forgive myself for letting anyone or anything harm me.

I forgive myself for withholding the Love I Am.

I forgive myself for forgetting to forgive it all.

How Does Life Work?

I am awake and aware and create with wisdom and love.

My life works for me, because I do the work.

I create only Goodness, wholeness and Love for All.

No Complaints

I now stop complaining or telling unhappy stories about life.

I choose to always and only share what is positive, creative and inspiring.

I use words wisely to create exactly what I want or something better.

I immediately erase, delete, forgive and release all that is not good for me.

Our Greatest Fear May Be Love!!

Love is freedom and Trust.

Love is letting go of fear.

Love is trusting and choosing the Highest Good.

Love is letting life be as it is.

Welcome Love in Your Life!

I release all fear of loving and being loved.

Loving and being loved is safe, fun and easy.

I now recognize and clear all blocks to giving and receiving Love.

Love opens the way to inner peace, happiness, health and prosperity.

Does Anybody Really Care?

I care about taking good care of myself and all my relationships.

I care about taking good care of my home, my workplace, my community and the earth.

I care about speaking and behaving with respect and kindness all the time.

I care about being the best example of conscious living that I know.

Love Is A Decision I Must Make.

I choose for Love.

I make the decision to Love, only Love.

I forgive and Love everyone who forgets to Love.

I remember Love is what we're here for.

Life Works When You Work Joyfully at Life!

I always have plenty of energy to do what I love.

There is always enough of everything I need to live my life with joy and gratitude.

Life works for me and with me, because I enjoy and appreciate life.

I spend everyday in celebration and appreciation of all that I have and do and give.

I love my life and life loves me.

Let's Get Real!

I live my life effectively and successfully.

I trust I am where I need to be doing what is mine to do.

My relationships are harmonious, my work is fulfilling and I love myself well.

I live my life and learn with wisdom, ease and grace.

Fear and Love

Life is Good and getting better.

I choose to live with loving and peaceful thinking and speaking.

I forgive quickly and receive the blessings instantly.

I learn from everything and everyone ONLY LOVE IS REAL.

Stop…. Breathe….. Step Away

I no longer need approval from others. I now approve of myself.

I am highly pleasing to myself in the presence of _____.

I trust and respect myself, therefore I treat others with trust and respect.

The more I respect myself and others, the more they learn to respect me.

I control my emotions by choosing the thoughts I think.

I behave as a responsible and respectful adult with self control and self discipline.

Assistance From Reunion

We are willing to help you turn around your negative programming or anything you continue to believe about lack or limitation.

1.   We ask you to send us your current belief, your current negative position.

2.   Make a statement about wanting to change your mind and be free of limited thought. For example: "I want to change my mind and think thoughts for my Highest Good."

3.   We shall use the guidance of Spirit and co-create healing affirmations for you to clear the way to conscious abundant living which you so richly deserve.

4.   Send whatever donation your heart wants to contribute to our ministry.

Reunion Ministries

17664 Greenridge Road

Hidden Valley Lake, CA 95467

(800) 919-2392

Personal Affirmations

Personal Affirmations

Personal Affirmations

Betty Lue Lieber, Ph.D.

Born August 16, 1942 in Michigan

Living in Hidden Valley Lake, California

Holy Union, life partner with Robert Waldon since 1985

Mother of two daughters + step daughter and son.

Grandmother of eight

Spiritual partner, guide and mentor to hundreds.

Founder of Reunion, Forum for Global Holistic Spirituality

Founder of 22 Counseling-Healing Centers in 5 states

Director of Reunion Living Ministry Program

CA Licensed Marriage and Family Therapist since 1977

Whole Life Coach and Success Consultant

Natural Health Educator

Feng Shui Practitioner/Teacher

Certified T'ai Chi Chih Teacher

Ordained Interfaith Reunion Minister

Co-Minister of Unity Center for Inspired Living

Doctorate in Theocentric Psychology

Masters in Clinical and School Psychology

Betty Lue's Teachings as a Child

We are whole.

We are not lacking or limited.

We are here to be helpful.

We are born to be happy.

We are born to be loving.

We are free and unrestricted.

We need no criticism or praise.

We are right within our Self.

We are trustworthy and trusting.

We are honest and open.

We are generous and share everything of value.

We value what is real and lasting.

We are patient as we learn from everything.

We are to love everyone equally.

We are here to follow Love and our Inner Truth.

There is nothing to fear.

There is complete innocence, as all are children.

There is nothing that cannot be forgiven.

All paths lead to Good and God.

All things are possible.

Love gives us everything we ask for the sake of Loving.

Miracles are natural.

We are all in the family of man and everyone is our brother.

God is Love and we are the loving creation of God.

Healing comes from the release from guilt and fear.

Reunion Ministries

Reunion Ministries was a gift from Spirit for me and those I have worked with over the last 37 years. Reunion, a non-profit church without walls, organization without requirements, programs without evaluation, spirituality without dogma, is a forum for all to explore their own beliefs, to heal their hearts and open to Spirituality within their own lives. These precepts are the guidelines through which we grow together in Trust and Freedom, the essence of Love ItSelf.

Precepts of Reunion

We are all Spiritual Beings.

All life is inter-connected.

Love is our natural state and the unifying force of all creation.

To create what is good, beautiful & whole is our call.

Forgiveness and freedom from judgment and fear bring healing and love.

All relationships bring us into conscious awareness of our blocks to love and our healing needs.

We are here to learn & teach what we are learning.

We respect all Beings, honor all Paths.

We listen within and serve the Highest Good for All.

A Forum for Global Holistic Spirituality

Reunion offers the space of freedom & trust in which to:

1. Reclaim our True Self.

2. Actualize our full potential.

3. Balance our relationship with all life.

4. Live our vision of cooperation and co-creation.

Mastery of Reunion

My intention is to inform, inspire and invite you to join with me in whole life integration and inner REUNION.

1. *Align mind, body and Spirit.*

2. *Honor heaven and earth.*

3. *Balance home and work.*

4. *Explore real work and recreation.*

5. *Give yourself quiet & interactive time.*

6. *Realize connectedness with all life.*

7. *Accept human differences.*

8. *Respect all life.*

9. *Know harmony and unity, inside and outside.*

This is truly the mastery of Inner Reunion.

Betty Lue Offers

Consultations:
By phone, Skype, email, home or office.
Phone: **800-919-2392** voicemail/pager
Email: **bettylue@reunionministries.org**
Home: 17664 Greenridge Rd., Hidden Valley Lake, CA 95467
Offices:
Reunion Center for Counseling, Healing and Growth
3496 Buskirk Ave, #103 Pleasant Hill, CA 94523
Unity Center for Inspired Living
50 Sand Creek #140, Brentwood, CA 94513
Holistic Center for Inspired Living,
50 Sand Creek, #320, Brentwood, CA 94513
Positive Living Center
17568 Spruce Grove Ext, Hidden Valley Lake, 95467

Reunion Living Ministry Program
See ReunionMinistries.org

Experiential training for those who seek to focus and facilitate
their spiritual development, life purpose and calling.

Workshops and Retreats— See **Loving Reminders.org**

Email your request for annual schedule of programs.

Daily Loving Reminders
Receive by email—*bettylue@reunionministries.org*
View on the web at *www.lovingreminders.org*

.

Books published	Coming soon
Loving Reminders	*Family Reminders*
Peaceful Reminders	*Healthy Reminders*
Relationship Reminders	*A Child's Reminders*
Pocketbook of Affirmations	*Success Reminders*
Healing Reminders	*Happiness Reminders*

Love Heals

&

Makes all things new.

The only mistake we ever make

is when we forget to love.

Remember:

Love You.

Love God.

Love Everyone.

www.ingramcontent.com/pod-product-compliance
Lightning Source LLC
Chambersburg PA
CBHW060402050426
42449CB00009B/1862